The Immigrants' Children

An Oral History of Portland, Oregon's Early Jewish & Italian Neighborhood

Polina Olsen

Smart Talk Publications

Portland, Oregon

Copyright © 2012 Polina Olsen

All inquiries should be addressed to
Smart_Talk_Publications@comcast.net

ISBN: 0978718313

ISBN- 13   978-0978718312

Second edition.

DEDICATION

To my grandparents, all immigrants from Eastern Europe - Sol Greenspan, Sarah Lipitz, Sam Charloch and Polina Sklarsky

The author's grandfather Sol (standing) with his parents, brothers and sister in Liepaja, Latvia around 1900.

Table of Contents

Acknowledgments

My first thanks go to the many people I interviewed for this book: Norman Berlant, Deborah Reinhardt Brandt, Ernie Casciato, Frieda Cohen, Col. Joe Colasuonno, Carl Costanzo, Richard Falaschetti, Fred Granata, Leo Greenstein, Dr. Daniel Labby, Abby Gail Layton, Richard Matza, Jack Rosen, Mike Scorcio, Eloise Durkheimer Spiegel, Larry Spiegel, Jerry Stern, and Harry Turtledove. Special gratitude to Gussie Reinhardt, of blessed memory, for her help and encouragement, her humor and her wonderful stories.

I'd also like to thank Brian Johnson at the Portland City Archives and Neal Van Horn at the Portland Development Commission (PDC) for their help with photographs. Thank you, my friend, Myra Beetle, - your quiet encouragement came at just the right moments. Most of all, I'd like to thank my wonderful husband Andy for his unending help and support.

Introduction

South Portland before Barbur Boulevard replaced the interurban railway trestle. Courtesy Col. Joseph Colasuonno.

Jews and Italians settled in South Portland during the immigration wave of the early 1900s. Few Jews lived there before 1900 but by 1920 there were over 6,000. Around the same time, Portland's Italian population grew and by 1910 numbered over 5,500.

The immigrants established a self-contained community that replicated the societies they'd left in Europe. Jews had kosher butcher shops and bakeries, synagogues and a mikvah. Italians had ethnic food, bocce bal, and Saint Michael the Archangel, their beautiful Italian National Church.

The community extended roughly between Southwest Bancroft Street and Portland State University (please see the map on page 64). A series of highway projects and the 1960's South Auditorium Urban Renewal left only scattered fragments. Portland's aerial tram from South Waterfront to the Oregon Health Sciences University provides a view of many older homes and institutions mentioned in this book.

Although the neighborhood no longer exists, it still means a great deal to those who remember. This book tries to capture the spirit of daily life in South Portland through the words of the immigrant generation's children and grandchildren.

Meet the Immigrants' Children

Jack Rosen's parents 1910 marriage at Gevurtz Hall. The bride, Dinah Schneiderman, stands next to her mother, Dora. Jack's great-grandmother is left of Jack's father, the groom, Nathan Rosen. Courtesy Jack Rosen.

Immigrants' children and grandchildren provided the memories for this book. Many grew up in South Portland between the early 1900s and the 1950s. Interviews were conducted between 2004 and 2006.

Ernie Don Casciato (1954 -) teaches drama in the Portland Public Schools. His grandparents settled in South Portland, and his father grew up there.

My grandfather's brother was a foreman on the Columbia Gorge Highway project. He sent for my grandfather in 1907. Their town in Abruzzi, Italy was remote. When my great-grandmother joined them in 1922, she'd never seen a radio, phonograph, or telephone. She didn't even know who Caruso was.

Frieda Cohen, photo by author.

Frieda Gass Cohen (1920 -) grew up in South Portland as the youngest of five children. She graduated Reed College and started a business with her husband in 1946.

We lived in a three-story house at 926 SW Jackson St., and if you asked my children, they'd say it was the most beautiful house in the city. It lacked all modern conveniences with just one bathroom upstairs and a laundry in the basement. A lot of people took in boarders, and my mother rented out a back bedroom.

The highway commission took my parent's home to build a freeway.

Colonel Joseph Colasuonno (1920 – 2009) grew up working in his family's South Portland Italian grocery stores. He joined the U.S. Air Force in 1941 and retired a full colonel in 1969.

My grandfather came to Portland in 1897 and opened a saloon on Fourth Street near Duniway Park in South Portland. Later, he owned Garibaldi Grocery across the street from his old saloon.

The store was a headquarters for new Italian immigrants. They listed it as their address and kept their valuables in Grandfather's safe.

During the Depression, the people hurting most were Italian. They lost their low-paying jobs and had large families to feed. My grandfather gave them credit and took care of them, especially old customers.

Carl Costanzo (1913 – 2013) grew up on Southwest Broadway Drive. His father, Nat Costanzo, was among Portland's earliest Italian settlers.

Carl Costanzo, Courtesy Patti Falaschetti.

South Portland was mostly Italian and Jewish. The Italians lived around what is now Duniway Park, and the Jews lived more toward First Avenue. We had one African-American named Flash, a German family, and Cottell who owned the drugstore.

The houses weren't big the way they are today. They had a basement, dining room, living room and kitchen. Some had the bathroom and bedrooms upstairs. My parents lived on Hall Street in South Portland until 1912 when they moved to the house my father built on Broadway Drive.

Richard Falaschetti (1943 -   ) is Carl Costanzo's nephew. A retired history teacher, he served as president of the local Order of the Sons of Italy. Mr. Falaschetti's immigrant grandparents settled and raised their family in South Portland.

Richard Falaschetti, Courtesy Patti Falaschetti.

My maternal grandfather was an upper-class Italian. Many Italian immigrants couldn't read or write but Nat Costanzo taught himself. I have deeds going back to 1900 where he'd lent money and was paid back in property. If he'd kept it, we'd own land from Caruthers to OHSU.

With the Falaschettis, it was different. My father grew up near Duniway Park between Third and Fourth Avenue and Sherman. Their kitchen had a wood and electric stove and smelled like olive oil and garlic. I remember the old toaster. My grandfather, Emilio Falaschetti, made toast and soft-boiled eggs every morning. First, he worked in a sawmill along the river but later he bought an Italian restaurant on the east side and worked as the chef.

The houses around Duniway Park were old and wood-framed and always smelled like something was burning. Many were built on 30-foot lots. The front door opened to the living/dining room combination with two bedrooms to the right. The living room led to the kitchen, bathroom and steps going down into a cellar which had one of those lift-up doors to the back yard. My grandfather smoked those little Turkish cigars down there and then had a glass of brandy.

I grew up on Southeast Sixty-Seventh and Woodward Street. Most eastside Italians lived in the Tabasco area particularly around Ladd's Addition. They moved from South Portland because they were farmers in the old country and wanted more land.

Fred Agostino Granata (1931 – 2010) was a Portland attorney and local Italian history expert. His parents grew up in South Portland.

We visited my aunt's house in South Portland almost every weekend. They'd bring out a meal and then the adults ate fruit and nuts and played cards until the next meal.

We lived at Southeast Fifty-Eighth Avenue and Bush. There weren't many Italians in our neighborhood but further west there were, especially around St. Ignatius Church. The two places Italians lived were South Portland and the close-in eastside.

Leo Greenstein (1920 – 2011) grew up in South Portland and became a Certified Public Accountant.

We lived in a typical South Portland house – small, one story, two bedrooms, and a dirt basement. Nothing special about it. My parents stayed there until they died.

Our house was a haven for lonely people. Back in the olden days, people dropped in. They didn't call and ask if they could come over. My father sat on the front porch, and people walked by, stopped, and came up. My mother gave them tea and cookies.

Dad went to citizenship school when he first came over, and my mother went in the '30s. Most of their reading was in Yiddish, like the Jewish paper, the Forward. There were other Jewish publications -- quite a few from the Left. There was a strong Jewish socialist movement back east, and they sent speakers around the country. It was lively. That was the intellectual life.

Dr. Daniel Labby (1914 – 2015) spent his early years in South Portland and became a professor of internal medicine. His father was a South Portland dentist.

It was an Orthodox home on Southwest Second Avenue across from what is now Lair Hill Park. We lived with my grandparents until I was four and then moved five blocks away. Eventually we moved to the new area, Laurelhurst. There was some feeling of social progression.

My parents spoke English except to tell secrets but had parties where everyone spoke Russian. Men wore blouses with a collar, and everyone drank tea from the samovar and discussed events in Europe. Sometimes my father read Shalom Aleichem aloud in Yiddish.

Abby Gail Layton, Courtesy herself.

Abby Gail Layton (1949 -) grew up in Portland. A psychotherapist for 25 years, she founded Or Hadash, a Jewish meditation group. Her great-grandparents homesteaded in North Dakota before moving to South Portland.

Gussie Reinhardt told me stories about my grandmother, Ada, and her husband, Jacob Layton. They lived kitty-cornered from Kesser Israel Synagogue, and Jacob ran a large barrel company. As a child, Gussie walked by every day and saw Jacob working out with barbells. He bought the first car in the neighborhood and drove kids to the gorge or beach on weekends.

My father was the youngest of 11 children. He was a spiritual man and went into his adult life poor. He made a good living at his pillow and bedspread business and gave half his money to Temple Beth Israel.

Richard Matza, Courtesy himself.

Richard Matza (1947 -) was president of Congregation Ahavath Achim for many years and remains an active member. He grew up in South Portland during the 1950s.

My uncle owned two adjacent houses and a tavern. When my father arrived in Portland, he got a job at the tavern and moved into one of the houses.

My father came from a small, lakeside village in Greece called Jannina. A large oak tree grows in the middle of the main street and an old walled section remains. Plaques for townspeople who perished in the Holocaust hang on the synagogue wall. Our last name, Matza, appears on about 300 of those plaques.

These are Romaniote, not Sephardic Jews. Romaniotes are descendants of Jewish slaves taken by Romans after the Second Temple's destruction. They escaped into the Greek hills during a shipwreck. They speak Greek, not Ladino, and their customs and melodies are different.

For example, instead of facing the Torah, the seats and benches of the old synagogue in Jannina face sideways. My father absorbed the Spanish-Judaic culture that my mother and most non-Ashkenazi Jews shared. Still, on Passover he sang Had Gad Yah in Greek.

Gussie Reinhardt, Courtesy Jewish Review.

Gussie Kirshner Reinhardt (1908 – 2005). The Grande Dame of Portland's Jewish community, Gussie Reinhardt grew up a few doors from Kesser Israel Synagogue where her father served as president for 40 years. After graduating from the University of Washington, she danced with the Martha Graham Company in New York. She returned to Portland after WWII and actively contributed to the Jewish community and to local politics.

Mama and Papa came from villages near Odessa, and they married in Russia. My father's uncle lived in Salem since 1864, and in 1903 my father joined him. We moved to Portland when I was 10 months old.

It's still sharp in my memory. We lived in a little house on the corner of Southwest Third Avenue and Meade Street. Our barn next door housed the junk peddler's horses and wagons.

Around 1924 the Jews started moving out of South Portland. Mama never wanted to leave but the ravine next to us became the local garbage dump.

Deborah Reinhardt Brandt (1945 -) is Gussie Reinhardt's daughter. She is a physical therapist and lives in New York City.

The neighborhood around Kesser Israel hasn't changed much since the '50s, except for the condominiums. It was a quiet area with the Neighborhood House, Lair Hill Park, the museum library, and tiny one- and two-story houses.

My mother's house was a rental when I saw it. It was a small, gray, cement home with little rooms, low ceilings and small windows. The barn was a huge, wooden structure built over a gulch. It had large doors which were usually open and a wood plank driveway.

Jack Rosen with his family. Courtesy Jenn Director Knudsen.

Jack Rosen (1920 – 2007**)** grew up in South Portland and became the women's wear buyer at Meier & Frank.

My grandmother had a grocery store called Schneiderman's on the corner of Southwest First Avenue and Hall, across from the Shaarie Torah Synagogue. She gave it to my parents when they married. It was a typical store with large windows, and we sold produce. The store was a meeting place, too. My father read the Bintel Brief, and men sat around on apple boxes and discussed it.

Our living quarters were first behind the store and then upstairs. The furniture was early Depression period, and we had pictures on the walls especially of relatives left in Europe. It was an Orthodox, kosher home where the shochet came and killed chickens in the basement. My parents tried to speak English and only told secrets in Russian.

Mike Scorcio (1920 – 2014) grew up in South Portland. He served as a WWII Air Force pilot, and later worked for the Houston Chamber of Commerce.

Mike Scorcio's 1937 Benson High graduation photo. Courtesy himself.

My father came from a small town in Southern Italy near Sannicandro. I visited twice, once during the war.

When Dad came to America in 1907 he had three objectives: learn to read, become a citizen, and vote. It was 1935 before he became a citizen, 28 years after he arrived. He did his best though -- he was tough. I remember one incident during the Depression when he went down to the commissioner's court. He jumped over the counter and said, "I don't want charity, I want a job."

When Dad came to Portland, he lived in a boarding house in Linton, and my 17-year-old mother lived there, too. Her father had a husband picked out for her but she saw my dad. So, my mother made the decision to marry my father, which was unusual.

Our house was on the corner of Southwest Hood and Whitaker. Italian families were scattered around, and our aunt, uncle, cousins, grandmother and other relatives lived close by.

I remember my godmother. Every Christmas she gave me an orange stuffed with coins. In 1927, my grandmother and godmother gave me money for Christmas so I had $3.00. I opened an account at the U.S. National Bank.

Eloise Durkheimer Spiegel (1923 – 2015) grew up in Northwest Portland. Her grandfather, Julius Durkheimer, was an early German Jewish settler. He owned general stores in Eastern Oregon and became Mayor of Burns in 1895.

Young Jewish men often went into the hinterlands, made their fortune, and moved back to the city. My grandfather, Julius, opened a general store in Burns. One time he closed the store for Rosh Hashanah but the Indians didn't understand it was temporary and started an uprising. The next Rosh Hashanah he closed the store again but this time he had someone stand guard.

Jerry Stern (1926 – 2015) grew up in South Portland and founded a plumbing distribution business. Active in local and national Jewish organizations, Mr. Stern served on the HIAS Board of Directors for 25 years. He helped Soviet and Iranian Jews settle in the United States, including several family members.

Jerry & Helen Stern, Courtesy Jerry Stern.

We lived a block away from my father's garage, on the corner of Southwest Fifth and Lincoln. My father cut a passageway between his two adjacent houses. First, a grandmother and uncle lived in the second house and later an aunt, uncle and cousins came. It was like one big house. We went into each other's iceboxes.

We knew everyone in our neighborhood, and everyone knew us. You didn't do anything wrong because the whole community would hear about it, and you'd be shamed. Growing up in the primitive area of South Portland in poverty, I don't think anyone ended up in jail.

Harry Turtledove (1921 – 2011) was a sportswriter for the Oregon Journal during the 1940s and later worked as a freelance journalist in Europe. He returned to Oregon in 1952 and founded a Portland advertising agency. His parents and grandparents lived in South Portland.

I never lived in South Portland, my parents did. I lived in Vancouver until I was five, and then we moved to Northeast Portland around Thirty-fourth and Hancock Street.

The neighborhood was lower- and middle-class single-family homes. In retrospect, it was rather simple but one didn't know it at the time. Ethnically it was Waspish. One Jewish family lived on our block for a couple years until the father went to prison.

My grandmother lived a few blocks from us. Every Sabbath she walked downtown, picked out a live chicken, and took it to the shochet in South Portland to be properly executed. After that she brought it home, and I got to help pull out the feathers.

My parents frequently drove to South Portland to buy things like herring from barrels and matzoh. They left South Portland for better housing and more assimilation into the larger community. It didn't mean they gave up being Jewish. This was the first generation where English was the native language so they didn't feel the insecurity that comes when you can't speak properly. They moved out because they'd reached a degree of affluence and didn't have to live in South Portland.

Coming to Portland

A Russian Jewish Immigrant Family. Courtesy Ruth Saltzman.

The immigrants' children cited several reasons for their ancestors' immigration to America but the most common were avoiding conscription and economic hardship. Some families had friends or relatives in Portland.

About 400 Jews came to Oregon under the auspices of the Industrial Removal Office. Trustees of the Baron de Hirsch Fund founded this New York based organization in 1900. Hoping to ease slum conditions and prevent anti-immigrant legislation, they relocated unemployed Jewish workers who volunteered to move from New York's Lower East Side to Jewish communities throughout the United States.

IRO agents from New York visited and recruited local agents from Jewish communities around the country. They lent settlers money for train tickets and supplemented the local agency's budget. From 1905 to 1917, Ben Selling was Portland's IRO agent. With the help of the Hebrew Benevolent Association, he found work and housing and then notified New York that a place was available. Recruits with relatives in Portland could come without a job guarantee. They frequently became junk peddlers with money for a horse and wagon lent to them by the Hebrew Benevolent Association.

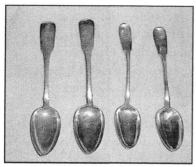

Oscar Kirshner left Russia with these silver spoons in case border guards demanded a bribe. Courtesy Deborah Reinhardt Brandt.

Deborah Reinhardt Brandt: My grandfather played the coronet in the Czar's army. He made a pact with my grandmother that when his number came up to fight, he would escape. He left with four silver spoons to use as bribes and with his tefillin which he wrapped around his head when he swam across a river. He went around the Black Sea, and took a boat to America.

He kept the spoons in the kitchen table drawer and counted them every day. I still have them.

Leo Greenstein: Stories of the old country were about poverty. My parents were from Belarus, and both were orphans. My dad's parents lived in a little village with few Jews so they sent him to a Beth Midrash. He slept there and ate at a different home every night.

After her mother died and her father remarried, my mother lived with various relatives and worked in a factory making matches. They gave her a stool to stand on. My parents said as a whole the Russians weren't bad but they were awfully poor. Dad said the only time they had fear was around Easter and Christmas when the priest harangued people.

Ben Selling might have been the one who helped my father. The immigrants didn't know who helped them but they knew someone did. Dad had to sneak across the border to avoid the Russian draft but fortunately there was graft. He got the ticket in Bialystock, went through Austria, Switzerland, France and Belgium and finally got an English ship to Quebec. From there he joined four aunts in South Portland.

My mother came on a German ship to Baltimore, joined family in Minneapolis and then a sister in Portland.

Harry Turtledove: My maternal great-grandfather was kidnapped as a child into the Czar's army and served out his 20-year term. When he left, he got a Golden Medina. This meant he could travel freely in Russia and, unlike most Jews, could live in Moscow. He became a lumber merchant. He sent his two sons to England to prevent their conscription, and he never saw them again.

One son, my grandfather, was a cabinetmaker. He had kidney disease, and the story is the king's physician said he needed a dry climate. They went to Oakland, California, where he worked for the railroad and my grandmother made wigs for Orthodox ladies. Oakland was too rough so in escaping England for a drier climate, they came to Portland, Oregon.

Grandfather ended up owning a clothing store. Wealthy Jewish businessmen called him when they changed suits. He picked up, cleaned, and re-sold their old ones. When Meier and Frank had new suits on sale their buyer took the labels out and sold them to Grandfather on commission.

The store was on Southwest Third Avenue and Burnside, which was a rough area, but not like today. Logging camps closed during the winter, and men came with their season's earnings. They got cheap rooms, drank a lot and so forth.

Frieda Cohen: My father was not about to serve in the Czar's army. He couldn't live in Moscow, he couldn't go to a Russian school, he couldn't own land and he couldn't own a business. He could only die for the Czar. My parents emigrated in 1907.

They lived in New York City the first two years. My father bought a sewing machine and carried it 10 miles to save the nickel subway fare to the garment district. Sometimes, the boss had him sit around until noon before saying there was no work. By then it was too late to go to a competing company.

They hated New York and the dirty tenements. My mother had a sister living in Portland whose husband was a cabinetmaker. It took my parents five days to get here by train, and they found a place to rent in South Portland.

My father opened a tailor shop from the trade he'd learned in New York. He went to work for Metropolitan Life Insurance just before the Depression and stayed until 1949. He spoke impeccable English, read everything, and knew history and politics better than college professors.

Mike Scorcio: You'd go into the Italian army. Well, my father didn't want that. He emigrated in 1907 with the $35 his family collected.

My mother's family came in 1914 during WWI. They closed the steerage-class curtains so German submarines couldn't see the lights. Her dad came to the U.S. eight years earlier and finally sent for his family. He had a shoe-making business on Sixth Street in South Portland.

They came to Portland because acquaintances from Italy were here. People went where they knew others of the same nationality. It was regional. Baris hung around with Baris, Tuscans with Tuscans, Neapolitans with Neapolitans.

Several Jewish communities and individual homesteaders farmed in North Dakota. One group left together and settled in Portland.

Leo Greenstein: My aunt and her husband homesteaded in North Dakota. It didn't last long. It was awful. He worked for the railroad somewhere while my mother's sister and her kids stayed on the prairie. They said North Dakota was horribly cold -- worse than Russia. Once they had a fire going and a wolf stuck his nose in the door just to warm up.

Ada Calof, Courtesy Abby Gail Layton.

Abby Gail Layton: They didn't talk about North Dakota but I've read the book, "Rachel Calof's Story." She was the mail order bride from Ukraine who married my great-grandfather's brother. My great-grandparents came from Poland and tried homesteading in Ontario before moving to North Dakota. They came to Portland when my grandmother, Ada Calof, was three years old.

Ada became a big, strong woman. She weighed close to 300 pounds, and nobody messed with her. She stood up for the Jewish people in South Portland like if someone bullied a kid. She also did civic work like going door-to-door for the Red Cross.

My mother's side is from Vancouver, Canada where her great-grandfather taught Chinese immigrants kosher cooking. Her grandparents went to California during the Gold Rush and sold Levi jeans.

In 1891, the Baron de Hirsch Fund founded a Jewish agricultural community in Woodbine, New Jersey which included the Woodbine Agricultural College, schools and factories.

Daniel Labby: My father and grandfather came to America first and sent for my grandmother and the remaining six children. Grandfather's friend from the shtetl lived in Portland, and eventually our whole family made it out here. My father got into dental school and sent for my mother who was a nurse in New York. They married in Portland and lived in my grandparent's house on Southwest Second Avenue.

My parents met at Woodbine. You know Woodbine? It was a center for immigrant Jews because of two things: First, the agricultural school founded by Baron de Hirsch. They thought so many Jews were peasants that at least they could make a living farming. The second reason was Mr. Uditsky. Grandfather learned hat making in his factory.

When Grandfather came to Portland he opened a hat store but the men sat around discussing Midrash which wasn't great for business. Eventually, he became shammes at Shaarie Torah.

Several of the immigrant's children told how their parents or grandparents arrived in New York and got jobs with the railroad. Sometimes they settled in Portland because they found themselves at the end of the line.

Harry Turtledove: My paternal grandfather immigrated to Canada about 1884 and worked on the trans-continental railroad. He took a sled and some trinkets and went trading with the Indians. When he had enough money, he sent for my grandmother in Romania.

My father was born in Winnipeg, and his family moved to Minneapolis, San Francisco, and finally Portland around 1904. The Minneapolis, San Francisco, Portland route was common, by the way.

Grandfather worked in the transfer or moving business. He was an independent, self-taught man who spoke several languages. He was involved in Jewish affairs and was a founder of the Beneficial Aid Society, out of which the Robison Center grew.

Carl Costanzo: They had real poverty in Italy. When my father, Nat Costanzo, was about 20, he and his brother came to America. They landed at Ellis Island. When Dad found out the railroad company was laying tracks, he got a job and worked with them all the way to Portland.

Ernie Casciato: My maternal grandfather, Ernesto Apa, was born in 1892. He was the youngest of nine children and from a small village on a steep hill in Calabria. In those days, Italy was a serfdom. His family had a plot of land and had to give so much to the Dom.

When he was 16, he left Italy alone and joined relatives in Toronto. He worked as a cook in lumber camps and met my grandmother when he stopped in Portland to visit relatives. They lived in South Portland when they first married but moved near St. Philip's [2408 SE 16th Ave.] where a lot of Sicilians lived.

Richard Falaschetti: My grandfather, Nat Costanzo, emigrated from Italy in 1894 and worked his way across the U.S. to Portland with the railroad. He went to Alaska, and in 1899 returned to Portland with $50,000. In 1912, he built a house on 811 SW Broadway Dr. for $20,000. The basement alone had a wine cellar worth $30,000 today.

After Nat Costanzo made his fortune in Alaska, he returned to Portland and built this house on Southwest Broadway Drive. Courtesy Richard Falaschetti.

The People of South Portland

*A South Portland family from Russia sits on
their front stoop. Courtesy Nina Weinstein.*

South Portland was about one-third Jewish, one-third Italian and
one-third everyone else including Irish, African-American, Greek
and Roma (Gypsies). The Jews in South Portland were Sephardim
or from Eastern Europe.

Everyone interviewed emphasized how well the different
groups got along. Several also mentioned how people of that
generation often stuck to their own kind. They attributed this to
differences in language and custom.

Leo Greenstein: In those days, eccentricities were considered more normal. Nowadays our education polishes us. We've mostly become Anglo-Saxons but at that time everyone was kind of different. People got angry and had colorful curses that we don't use anymore. People still had mannerisms from the little towns they came from.

Most of the Jewish people were from Ukraine. Some like my parents were from White Russia - Belarus, and a few were from Hungary and Romania. We had Sephardic people in our neighborhood but we were hardly aware of it although I knew they didn't speak Yiddish.

Mike Scorcio: My parents knew some Jewish families who lived close by. There was some exchange of visits particularly around Christmas. On Friday nights, my brother and I built one family's fire. They couldn't touch money on the Sabbath so they slipped 15 cents and something to nibble on under the tablecloth.

Richard Matza: Sephardic Jews, mostly from Turkey, went to Seattle around 1901. The climate was good, and the fishing was similar to the Mediterranean. As the community grew, some relocated to Portland.

Most Sephardic Jews lived in South Portland, and they all spoke Ladino. What they did in Turkey echoes what they did here. They shined shoes, had fruit and vegetable markets, sold fish, and owned taverns. They were small business people, and they eked out a living.

Frieda Cohen: In that generation, Sephardic Jews did not mix with the Yiddish speaking because their languages were different. They also had their own synagogue and customs.

Richard Falaschetti: My grandmother lived around Fourth and Sherman. Her best friend, Becky, was a Sephardic Jew. Grandmother came over to the U.S. in the early 1900s and spoke broken English. I could barely understand her but Becky could.

Fred Granata: The two places Italians lived were South Portland and the close-in eastside. The Tuscans tended to live off Hawthorne between Seventh and Twelfth Avenue and Sicilians lived east of there. South Portland was a mixture of northern and southern Italians but you have to realize that 80 percent of Italian immigrants were from the south. They had more reasons to leave Italy.

Leo Greenstein: A black family named Gray lived in that row of old houses on Second Avenue. One of the boys became a boxer. They had smokers -- little clubs that put on Friday night boxing shows. Some Jewish boys did that for a while.

Joe Colasuonno: Gypsies lived in an empty building across from my grandfather's store. Blankets divided the different families but they all cooked in one area.

Richard Matza: Several Gypsy families lived in South Portland when I went to Shattuck School in the '50s. One became a close friend. Toby's house was average middle class but his cousins' homes were an adventure. They lived in storefronts around Second Avenue and Jefferson Street, and two or three families separated their sleeping quarters with screens. The area close to the window was like a living room.

Toby left school in the spring and returned in the fall because his family operated game booths on the carnival circuit. His father was enterprising and worked for himself the rest of the year. He sold store signs that said things like Closed or Open, and sometimes he peddled carnival trinkets. All the Gypsies I knew bought and sold used cars.

Daniel Labby: The Gypsies were swarthy people, handsome men and beautiful women, and they dressed dramatically and spoke their own language. They lived in empty storefronts and whitewashed the windows or hung sheets for privacy. They always came to state fairs and told fortunes.

When someone died, they'd put on a big funeral cortege through the city. I think the King of the Gypsies died, and they all dressed up and paraded around in their beautiful clothes. It was summer, and the men still wore cashmere overcoats.

The Established German Jews

Congregation Beth Israel. Courtesy Oregon State Historic Preservation Office, 1997, Oregon Dept. of Transportation photographer Orrin Russie.

Few or no Jews from Germany lived in the South Portland neighborhood. They first arrived in Oregon after the 1849 California Gold Rush and settled in three major towns, Jacksonville, Albany and Portland. Many opened general stores in small Eastern Oregon towns and later returned to Portland where they mainly lived in Nob Hill or Portland Heights. They belonged to the Reform Movement of Judaism and attended Temple Beth Israel.

By the time Eastern European immigrants came, the German Jews had assimilated into mainstream America. While cultural and social differences remained until the next generation, the German Jews helped the newcomers both as individuals and through their organizations.

Eloise Durkheimer Spiegel: My family is of German Jewish descent. My grandparents were formal people who came to Oregon from Pennsylvania. When they came for dinner once a week, Grandpa gave each of us children a silver dollar to bank at school. Other children came with a penny or nickel but it didn't occur to us that we were different.

Our house was at 2522 NW Northrup St. We had lots of hired help. There was the live-in cook and maid and people to polish floors, do laundry, and take care of the garden. My father had a wholesale grocery, Wadhams & Company, and he belonged to the Tualatin Country Club.

Many German Jews from that generation felt a certain snobbery about the fact. They felt they were here first and were better educated and more polished. In Beth Israel Sunday School, there was little effort to meet children from other synagogues.

There were also religious differences. Reform Jews weren't kosher and could eat pork or milk with meat. They didn't have a B'nai Mitzvah either but they did go through confirmation class.

Later on, some German Jews felt the State of Israel was wrong. I remember the rabbi pointing out what a wonderful thing it was to have a place to go if the need arose but they didn't see it that way. They felt their Judaism closely but believed it was their own private business. To them, Judaism was a religion, and there shouldn't be a nation of just Jews.

Kishinev, the capital of Bessarabia, was the scene of a bloody pogrom in 1903. When a Christian child was found dead, the Jews were accused of blood libel or killing the boy to use his blood for Passover matzoh. Although relatives were found guilty of the crime before the pogrom started, the population murdered, injured and destroyed the homes of hundreds of Jews while officials turned a blind eye.

Appeals to help the victims went out around the United States. The locally published Jewish Tribune carried a letter from the American Federation of Zionists, and Neveh Zedek Talmud Torah Synagogue called a citywide meeting. The New York Times reported that the Jews of Portland contributed $5,000 to the relief effort.

Harry Turtledove: My father, who had total recall, told a story. It was 1903 right after the Kishinev pogrom.

He and his father went to the first citywide gathering of all Jews. This was a big deal. My grandmother would not quite call Reform Jews goyim but it wasn't far removed. So, in 1903 it took a tremendous emergency to get a citywide community gathering. Dad swore a speaker stood up and said, "We Jews," meaning German, "have called you Jews," meaning Polish, "to talk about what we're going to do for those Jews," meaning Russian. That seems like an extreme statement but essentially that was it.

Jerry Stern: German Jews came to Portland in the late 1800s and were business people. They spoke English, were better educated, and lived in Portland Heights. We went to high school with these kids and had wonderful relationships during the day but they didn't invite us to their homes. Then they were of a different world but today we're all the best of friends.

Leo Greenstein: Most German Jews came after the Gold Rush. There was no social interaction between German and other Jews but the German Jews helped a lot. It wasn't until my generation that the differences disappeared

Growing Up

The South Parkway basketball team met at the Neighborhood House. Circa 1930s. Courtesy Dr. Larry Mudrick.

The Immigrants' Children say South Portland was like a small-town where everyone knew everyone, and everything was within walking distance. Children played in the streets or parks, went to Failing or Shattuck school, and attended a neighborhood synagogue or church. Children watched cowboy movies at local theaters, community centers sponsored sports teams, and the Neighborhood House even provided a Hebrew School on the top floor.

Daniel Labby: As I rode by their stores on my tricycle, the owners phoned my mother to say, "I just saw Danny." I passed

Mosler's Bakery and Calistro & Halperin's delicatessen and ended up at Martell's grocery on Second Avenue. A small Turkish synagogue with the usual half-moon signature stood on the opposite side of the street.

We bought semichka [sunflower seeds]; We'd put them in our mouth and eat them coughing and spitting out the hull. We'd flatten pennies on the streetcar tracks and make chewing gum from the scooped-up tar.

A print shop near Failing School sold penny candy as a sideline. One day, I spotted something I didn't think was possible -- marzipan strips of bacon. I was sitting on the front steps of my grandfather's house eating them when he and my father came home. They were horrified. Of course, it turned into a big joke.

Jerry Stern: This was a typical day starting at about age nine. I walked the mile from school to downtown Portland and sold newspapers on a corner from 3:30 to 6 PM. All the kids did. Then I walked home, guzzled my food, and walked one and a half miles to Hebrew school at the Neighborhood House. Hebrew school was an hour and a half every Monday, Tuesday, Wednesday and Thursday night and again on Sunday mornings. I went to services on Friday night and Saturday morning.

South Portlander Hal Boren outside Tom Stern's Fourth Street Garage. Courtesy Bonnie Boren.

Leo Greenstein: Years ago, every Jewish boy in Portland sold newspapers on the street. During the Depression, it was the only way to make a few dollars and go to school.

Jerry Stern: My father cried when I gave up my $15 a month newspaper job. We needed that money. Then I got an insurance investigation firm job for $25 a month, so it was OK.

Mike Scorcio: One uncle was a fruit peddler and had an old truck. On weekends, the whole tribe -- 12 or 15 people drove to the coast. If it rained, who cared? We rented a house, and everyone piled in.

The Kirshner children from back left Hymie, Ora, Isadore and Gussie. Courtesy Deborah Reinhardt Brandt.

Gussie Reinhardt: We played hopscotch and drew on the sidewalk. We'd go one, two, hop and turn around. We skipped rope and ran in while the rope was going over. After dinner we played kick-the-can on the corner outside Kesser Israel Synagogue.

Carl Costanzo: There were no clubs. The school couldn't afford it. We had jobs around the house so we usually went straight home. On weekends we walked in the hills above Broadway Drive and played softball and soccer in a field near our house. In later years, we went dancing at McElroy's Ballroom on Southwest Fourth and Main.

Neighborhood House at 3030 SW 2nd Ave. was the heart of the South Portland Jewish Community. Photographer unknown, original rendering by Doyle & Pattern Architects. Courtesy State Histoic Preservation Office.

Neighborhood House

Originally a sewing school, the National Council of Jewish Women founded the Neighborhood House in 1896. A.E. Doyle, a prominent Portland architect, completed the new building at Southwest Second Avenue and Woods Street in 1910.

Neighborhood House was the center of South Portland's Jewish Community. Immigrants found citizenship and sewing classes, a free clinic and dispensary, a kindergarten, community meeting rooms and recreation facilities. The Hebrew school on the top floor served all the synagogues in South Portland.

Jerry Stern: South Portland was really two South Portlands. One was north South Portland and the other was south South Portland. The division was Duniway Park which was a gulch at the time. If you lived in south South Portland, you went to Failing School and the Neighborhood House. That's where you swam, played basketball and did gymnastics. If you lived in north South Portland, as we did, you went to Shattuck School and the B'nai B'rith building for recreation. We all met at the Neighborhood House for Hebrew school, and we all went to Lincoln High.

Eloise Durkheimer Spiegel: Mother was in the Council of Jewish Women and the Beth Israel sisterhood. She was a volunteer sewing teacher at the Neighborhood House when Gussie Reinhardt was one of the little children. Mother didn't develop friendships with South Portland people but she knew she was helping.

Ida and Zerlina Loewenberg (seated) with their family. Courtesy John Trachtenberg.

Frieda Cohen: Ida Loewenberg, the Neighborhood House director, was austere, prim, proper, and very nice. She permitted one young law student to live downstairs. The janitor and his wife fed him.

Leo Greenstein My mother never had a chance for an education in Europe but she went to Americanization school at the Neighborhood House to become a citizen. She learned to read and write and a little about American history. The class was a couple of afternoons a week and was mostly Jewish and Italian women.

Jerry Stern: Everyday a boy picked up the young kids in his touring car and took us to the Neighborhood House kindergarten. Most children in that kindergarten are still my friends today.

H.I. Chernichowsky served as the Neighborhood House Hebrew School principal from 1931 to the early 1950s. Courtesy Marcia Ketzlach Gale.

Gussie Reinhardt: When I went to kindergarten at the Neighborhood House, Mama always put a big bow in my hair. We sat in a semi-circle, and the teacher sat in front. We played musical chairs, and there was a big table where we made handicrafts and paper chains for holidays. We sang, "Pease porridge hot, pease porridge cold, pease porridge in the pot, nine days old."

Frieda Cohen: Our Hebrew school had a picnic every year. We met at the Neighborhood House and took the streetcar to Peninsula Park. We spent the day swimming, having races and playing games. In the afternoon, our parents brought our lunches.

The South Parkway Lodge was a Neighborhood House club. They collected money for charity and organized activities like picnics and dances.

Leo Greenstein: The South Parkway Lodge put on a minstrel show every few years. It was really good. Motle Jermolowske used to sing. He was 13 or 14 and a big strong fellow. It was comical.

Manley Community Center

While the Neighborhood House was non-sectarian and all were welcome, many people thought of it as a Jewish facility. Italians and other non-Jews played basketball and had contacts there but they considered the Manley Community Center their own.

In 1912, the Women's Home Missionary Society organized the Manley Community Center, and it moved next to Failing School in 1929. Originally called the South Portland Settlement Center, or Mission House, its first location was Southwest First Avenue and Caruthers Street. According to a 1920 Neighborhood House newsletter, proselytizing and deliberately attracting Jewish children with candy, swings, and a kindergarten caused friction with the Jewish community. The article states: "That is why the Missionary Society of America always establishes their branches in districts that have a large Jewish population. To convert a Jew, in their opinion, is to rescue a soul straight from hell ..."

Mission House influence diminished after the Neighborhood House reopened its own kindergarten and understanding between the communities increased. Ironically, the original Mission House on Southwest First Avenue and Caruthers Street became the Linath Hazedek Synagogue.

Mike Scorcio: We all looked forward to the Manley Community Center. I remember getting my first vaccination there. We played basketball and put on plays. One summer we studied Mexico and prepared a Mexican dinner. At Christmas they had other activities including a pageant. I was a Wise Man. One time they sponsored a softball competition, and we went across the river which was quite an adventure.

B'nai B'rith

Completed in 1914, the B'nai B'rith Building on Southwest Thirteenth Avenue between Mill and Market Streets was a recreation facility for people in the northern end of South Portland.

Q.E.D. party. Courtesy Toinette Menashe.

Frieda Cohen: Queen Esther's Daughters met at the B'nai B'rith building. We had parties and dances and around 20 girls became close friends. We didn't do much dating until we were 17 or 18, and we stuck to boys our own age. Our parents would have objected strenuously had we dated older boys.

Richard Matza: Sephardic kids didn't have special clubs. We integrated with the others. We hung around and played basketball at the old Jewish Community Center until it was time for Hebrew school at the Neighborhood House.

*Ora Kirshner's Failing School class. The principal,
Miss Fannie Porter, is third row left. Courtesy
Gussie Reinhardt.*

Grades One through Twelve

South Portland had two public grade schools, Josiah Failing and
Shattuck. Failing School was originally built in 1882 on the corner
of Southwest First Avenue and Hooker Street. The new building
on Southwest Porter Street opened in 1913. Shattuck School was
built in 1914, and the structure became part of Portland State
University in 1969.

Lincoln High School served all of South Portland. Between
1885 and 1912, it was located at Southwest Fourteenth Avenue and
Morrison Street. In 1912, Lincoln High moved to the South Park
Blocks, and the structure is now PSU's Lincoln Hall.

Daniel Labby: Miss Porter was the principal of Failing
School. She was strict. When we assembled for a fire drill she'd
address the entire student body: "Come to school, do your lessons,
respect the teacher," and so on. She always wore black and was a big
woman.

My teacher, Miss O'Conner was a wonderful gray-haired lady.
She'd hold a ruler but just tap you on the wrist or hand.

Jerry Stern: One kid said something improper and was sent to Miss Porter who washed his mouth out with soap. His mother ran down there screaming, "You can hit him, but don't you dare wash his mouth out with traif."

Mike Scorcio: We walked four blocks up a hill to Failing School. When we went home for lunch, a lady played the piano in the hall while we marched out single file and no talking.

Fred Granata: My mother graduated Failing School in 1918 when she was 14 years old. Her name was Amalia Carlo but everyone called her Mollie.

St. Mary's Academy is the oldest private school in Oregon. It opened in 1859 in a small wooden building on Southwest Fourth Avenue between Mill and Market Streets. The original structure was demolished in 1970 when the school moved to its current location at 1615 SW Fifth Ave.

Richard Falaschetti: My father went to St. Lawrence grade school and Columbia Prep High, which is now the University of Portland. My mother went to St. Michael's Parish School and St. Mary's. She tried Lincoln High but only lasted one week. She loved the nuns. She was lost at public school.

Carl Costanzo: A lot of South Portland Italians went to St. Lawrence Church, and they had a school for boys. My Dad was involved when the Italians built St. Michael's so we went to church and school there.

Today, they'd close the school. We had four rooms with two grades in each. There was no electricity so when it got dark, we went home. The only heat was a big pot-bellied stove in each classroom. The toilet was at the end of the hall where there was no heat. When it froze up, we had a holiday.

The nuns were hard-nosed and weren't afraid to use the ruler. If you didn't study, they knew.

Parks

Lair Hill Park at Southwest Second Avenue and Woods Street is directly across from the Neighborhood House and next to the Carnegie library building. Named after William Lair Hill who purchased the land in 1868, it became the property of Charles Smith who built a mansion and pleasure garden on the site. In 1909, Mr. Smith donated the land and house to the city who converted the mansion into Multnomah County Hospital. After the hospital moved to Marquam Hill, the city demolished the mansion, and the land became a public park.

Leo Greenstein: We all went to Lincoln High. After school the Jewish kids had Hebrew school at the Neighborhood House. When we weren't in Hebrew school we played ball in the street, a vacant lot, or Lair Hill Park. The park had counselors during the summer but we organized our own games. I don't remember the girls playing with us. Girls did some stuff -- swings. The parents didn't participate. They were immigrant people, and they didn't have time.

Duniway Park has an interesting history. In 1914, the Oregonian reported plans to create a new park by leveling the Marquam Gulch with garbage. Known as the sanitary fill method, the city deemed this less expensive than an additional incinerator. Construction stopped when the stench became unbearable.

When the city gave South Portland first priority for a new park in 1916, construction resumed. By the time the park expanded in 1923, they again used the sanitary fill method, this time with odor control.

Carl Costanzo: When I was in grammar school, the train ran along Fourth Street to the center of Portland. A trestle went over the gulch at Duniway Park. Duniway Park was a huge, deep, hole in the ground. The city wanted a landfill so all of Portland's garbage trucks dumped there. That garbage is still fermenting. There are vents around where methane gas escapes. If you light a match, there's flames.

Mike Scorcio: The gulch near Duniway Park had the inter-urban streetcar above it, and we walked along the trestle where Barbur Blvd. is now. The kids played softball at Duniway Park or in the middle of the streets.

Ernie Casciato: They loved sports, played ball, and watched the Beavers at the old Vaughn Street stadium. After WWII, the two Italian softball teams played in Duniway Park. My father's team was called the Quackaroos because he went to the University of Oregon.

The Haunted Castle

Gussie Reinhardt: We believed in the Ouija board. That was magic. And, there was a haunted castle on the hill. It isn't so far up today but in those days it seemed right under the sky. We could almost see ghosts going in and out.

Ernie Casciato: My father and his friends climbed to the haunted castle when they were kids. Nobody knew who haunted it or why. They heard it was brought over from Europe, and they knew ghosts lived there. Haunted castle was even written on the window when, years later, my father drove me over to see it.

Fred Granata: The kids walked up the stairway on Broadway Drive to where the medical school is today. I remember walking across a gully. A castle above Sixth Street was supposed to be haunted but I didn't believe that stuff.

We played in empty fields around the city. Wild berries abounded. We cut trails through them with a stepladder and clippers.

My mother canned the berries and made pie all winter long. We lived cheaply but had delicious food

When the Carnegie Library opened in 1921, South Portland children moved books from the old library down the street to the new one. Photo from the Multnomah County Library 150 Years of Library History Gallery.

The Library

In 1921, Carnegie Foundation funds financed a new library at 2909 SW 2nd Ave. The city moved the original library building from First Avenue and Hooker Street to 116 SW Meade St. where it became a private residence.

Gussie Reinhardt: The old library moved two doors from Kesser Israel and became a private home. The new library was a beautiful little Italianate building that is still there.

When my sister was 12, she became Zerlina Loewenberg's assistant. Zerlina Loewenberg was the head librarian and her sister, Ida, was the Neighborhood House director. Those two Loewenberg sisters were fine people. That family gave a lot to South Portland.

Leo Greenstein: Oh, that was wonderful. The library was the greatest thing in South Portland. They had all kinds of books. They had a children's section and a section of foreign languages -- mostly, I think Jewish, Yiddish. I read adventure books and later got to the more complex stuff.

Summer at the Beach

Frieda Cohen: Seaside was upscale, and you had to be dressed. My mother couldn't afford to dress up five children so we went to Long Beach, Washington and lived in little cabins on the beach. We didn't even have a toilet in the house. After they took the train away we started going to Rockaway. Seven or eight families came together and rented cabins. We stayed from Tisha B'Av until Labor Day.

Isaac and Cacalie Gevurtz at the beach. Isaac Gevurtz (1850-1917) emigrated from Poland and owned a downtown furniture store. Courtesy Dr. John Gevurtz.

My mother paid $12 a week, and we had the best time ever. The first thing we did each year was remove the dishes and scrub the shelves [to kosher the kitchen]. We brought kosher meat and did all our own cooking. We made bonfires on the beach and toasted marshmallows and potatoes in the sand. The potatoes were sandy, gritty and delicious.

Gussie Reinhardt: Mrs. Robison, for whom the retirement center was named, had wealthy sons who bought her a beach house in Long Beach, Washington. She invited Mama and the family to live there every July. Mrs. Robison and Mama worked closely together for Jewish causes, especially Israel.

Eloise Durkheimer Spiegel: Every summer we went to my family's beach house in Seaview, Washington. My dad stayed home working but came down on weekends.

Somehow, the ocean wasn't as dangerous then, and I never heard about drowning. We called it going bathing. We also went berry picking, and my mother and grandmother made delicious jams.

Theater

Jack Rosen: Traveling Jewish actors came during Rosh Hashanah and Passover and put on Yiddish plays at the Swiss Hall. When I was 15, a troupe arrived minus their piano player who had run off with the money. My father let them stay in an apartment he owned, and I ended up accompanying them on the piano.

Frieda Cohen: We saw all the musicals that came, 42nd Street, everything. Hogie Carmichael was a great favorite and so were the Dorseys and Artie Shaw. Jantzen Beach was an amusement park with rides and a dance hall. All the big bands from around the country came there to play.

Ernie Casciato: My dad loved vaudeville, and his favorite act was a banjo player named Eddie Peabody. All the big bands played at McElroy's Ballroom and Jantzen Beach. We went dancing as we got older.

Since many South Portlanders couldn't read English, the old subtitled silent movies created a problem. In his oral history, now at the Oregon Jewish Museum, Jimmy Berg remembered how noisy the theater became as children read aloud to their parents and grandparents.

Harry Turtledove: My grandmother took me to the Lincoln Theater to see Ben Hur. I can't remember if it had subtitles but why else would she have taken me?

Jerry Stern: Jimmy Berg's father owned the First Avenue Theater. We called it Berg's theater. We all went especially on Saturday afternoons when there were free cowboy movies, vaudeville and a concert. Well, you wouldn't call it a concert exactly but there was an organ. Movies got to Berg's theater several years after they'd been downtown.

Jimmy Berg's sister became a singer for the Metropolitan Opera in New York. She began her career singing with the organist at her father's silent movie theater. When she got a job at Kelly's Beer

Parlor, a talent scout spotted her. Also a numerologist, he felt sure her name, Minnie Berg, added up to bad luck. Since Monopoly was a popular board game at the time, he worked out the spelling Mona Paulee.

Frieda Cohen: Minnie Berg lived one block from me. You could go by any day and Minnie was singing scales. She made it to the Metropolitan Opera in New York. Her father had silent screen movies with subtitles in English, and somebody sat playing the organ.

Dating

Richard Falaschetti: When single men arrived from Italy, they lived in boarding houses. The people at the boarding house helped find them a job, and after that they helped them find a wife. A lot of marriages were arranged, and this wasn't a big deal. There was little dating in those days.

Daniel Labby: The young rabbi established the Octagonal Club since Temple Beth Israel is an Octagon. It was the era of the big band, and they put on dances almost every weekend. Everyone from Bing Crosby to Harry James was crooning. Most young people I dated were from Sunday school or the Octagonal Club.

Religion

Gussie Reinhardt: I didn't go to the cheder and neither did my brothers. My parents thought we'd learn better if the rabbi came to the house where my mother could watch out for monkey business. He came two or three times a week. When my brothers finished their session, the teacher read the Torah to me and drew pretty flowers where he ended. He called my brothers the meal and me the dessert.

Leo Greenstein: My folks didn't belong to a synagogue but sometimes we'd go to services at the Robison Home [retirement center], and I went to Hebrew school.

Deborah Reinhardt Brandt: Zaydeh led the Passover service, and lots of people sat around the table. We were always starving, and the food was fantastic, especially Auntie Rae's knaidlach and chicken soup. Uncle Hymie was the biggest tease in the world. He stuck an egg in and out of his mouth while Zaydeh was saying prayers. Everyone cracked up.

Richard Matza: I didn't know the English names for food, I knew them in Ladino. In Spanish chicken is pollo, but we say giyena. Bamya is okra, yaprak is grape leaves and fedejos is vermicelli.

Gussie Reinhardt: It's what I call real gourmet food. At Shavous, Mama made delicious cottage cheese, potato, and squash knishes. Every filling had a different shape. She rolled and gently pulled the dough until it stretched across the whole table. My brother could hardly wait for those knishes to come out of the oven. He'd grab one and run, and when my mother turned her back he'd grab another.

I don't remember my brothers' Bar Mitzvahs. In those days they didn't make such a to-do. You had a Bar Mitzvah because you were a little Jewish boy and from then on you counted in the minyan.

Mike Scorcio: Holidays were wonderful. The kids played together, the men played cards, and food was always on the table. We wound up sleeping on the floor -- who cares?

For Christmas we had turkey or beef, and the women made homemade macaroni. Our salads were whatever was available in our garden, and we had bread, special dishes, and Italian cookies.

Christmas gifts? Non-existent! We needed that money to feed the family.

Fred Granata: Christmas Eve dinner was pasta made from baccala. They soaked it for a week to get rid of the salt. My mother made homemade ravioli, and we had good cookies indeed! The pizza cookie had raisins and nuts soaked in honey. It was out of this world. Pizelles were flat and looked like waffles. We loved it when they hid them but, of course, they could only hide them for so long.

Richard Falaschetti: We celebrated Christmas on Broadway Drive. It was always festive. My grandmother was a great cook and started baking weeks in advance. She made lasagna with baccala sauce from the saltiest codfish, and she made Italian cookies and pizza which is traditional. Everyone came and exchanged gifts.

Men who grew up in South Portland had a lunchtime reunion each week at a local sports bar. In front, Marvin Enkelis (left) and Judge Tony Casciato. Photo by author.

At Work

South Portland grocery probably belonging to Jack Rosen's grandmother.
Courtesy Mike Rosen.

This sample of occupations gives a feel for the neighborhood, and everyone enjoyed talking about the stores and people they remembered. Junk peddlers were a favorite topic probably because so many immigrants started life in America this way.

Leo Greenstein: My father was a junk peddler. He went around collecting old things and sold them to the junk dealers who had stores on Front Avenue. He woke up at seven, ate mush for breakfast, and then he'd harness up Bill, his horse, and the wagon. He'd go to houses or businesses and pick up things like bottles, sacks, copper and brass. Once in a while he found an antique and made a little more money.

People were a lot poorer. If they wanted to work around the house and needed new equipment, they went to a second-hand store. The dealers also sold to farmers and businessmen.

Gussie Reinhardt: My father had a barn where he housed the horses and wagons of the, well, I call them original recyclers but in those days they called them junk peddlers. There were 20 horses which was a big help because the peddlers paid maybe three dollars a month.

Joe Colasuonno: They looked like junk yards. There were piles of metal scattered around which they sold by weight. The doors were shabby like a barn and had big latches and locks.

Junk peddlers came through the neighborhood with their horse drawn wagon and bell. You offered them anything you wanted to throw out, and sometimes they gave you a little money. We also had an Italian knife sharpener who pushed a homemade cart with a big stone wheel down the street like a wheelbarrow. He sharpened knives by pedaling the stone wheel like a player piano.

Jerry Stern: Front Avenue was storefront after storefront of junk dealers. They sold plumbing, electrical stuff, nails and a little furniture. They also sold scrap to some refinery that melted it down.

Carl Costanzo: Fruit and vegetable peddlers were mostly Italian. We always bought produce from one who drove his truck through our neighborhood. An Italian knife sharpener went around with a wheel he operated with his feet.

Joe Colasuonno: Garibaldi Grocery was the old-type store with wooden floors and the smell of Italian foods. We sold Romano and Provolone cheese, salami, dried codfish, and barrels of green olives in brine. Coffee came in 50-pound green cans. My grandfather spoke only Italian, and most of his customers were Italian. Others weren't acquainted with the food.

I delivered groceries. Many houses in South Portland were three stories, and you walked up 50 steps before getting to the porch. Customers usually bought by the month and got 100-pound sacks of flour and sugar and five or six 20-pound boxes of macaroni. They

Korsun's Deli. Courtesy Portland City Archives, A2005-005.

bought maybe half a wheel of Romano grating cheese. That's about 25 pounds.

In 1936 my father started his own store, Colasuonno & Son, on Southwest Third Avenue between Madison and Jefferson. We all worked. My mother and father were there full time, and my sister and I came after school and on weekends. Although I was underage, I was considered a proprietor and could sell liquor behind the counter.

By that time things were changing. Children had grown and left home so quantities were reduced. Customers didn't need 100-pound sacks of flour. As the store educated people about Italian foods the clientele also changed. People stopped to buy liquor on their way home from work, and my dad explained what things were and how to cook them. Gradually our customers converted from mainly Italian to mainly American.

One Christmas my folks bought me an electric train, and I put it in our store window. It went under a tunnel made from nuts and through Olive Grove where I displayed olives. Champagne Lake was a mirror. All the kids stopped to watch the train go round-and-round.

Frieda Cohen: Korsun's delicatessen was on the corner of Southwest First Avenue and Caruthers. It was kosher, and he had all the foods people wanted. A barber worked across the street, and somewhere nearby were Calistro & Halperin's Delicatessen and Mosler's bakery.

Deborah Reinhardt Brandt: I never had bagels as good as Mosler's anywhere. They weren't sweet. They were hard, chewy basic bagels. You can't find them anymore.

On Sundays, we went to South Portland to buy kippered salmon and bagels and sometimes knockwurst or salami for a special breakfast.

Gussie Reinhardt: I ate Mrs. Neusihan's pickles but not from the barrel the way people did that walked by. And, you know, Mrs. Neusihan was Rabbi Fain's sister. They came from Russia. When he left Shaarie Torah, he came to Kesser Israel and unofficially served as our rabbi.

Leo Greenstein: Every ethnic group had a hall, and Gevurtz was the Jewish one. It was a corner building on Southwest Front and Gibbs with a store on the main floor and a hall upstairs. The Masons met there, too. Wintler's drugstore was across the street. That was a neighborhood institution with a soda fountain and emergency medical care. When they widened Front Avenue, they wiped it out.

Dr. Wolfe's barbershop was originally on Southwest First Avenue and Sherman Street but moved to the edge of the Marquam Gulch. One day the shop slid into the gulch, and the story has been part of Portland lore since.

Jerry Stern: First Avenue in Portland was like Delancy Street in New York City. There were butchers and little grocery stores, Mosler's Bakery and Dr. Wolfe's barbershop. In those days, not only did the barber cut hair and do shaves but he also put leeches on for different problems. Everyone had a story about how he was sitting in

Dr. Wolfe's chair having his hair cut when the store fell into the Gulch.

Daniel Labby: My father was a dentist, and his office was a curtained-off section of our living room. We lived on the second floor above Cottell's drugstore. There were two apartments, ours and one occupied by a series of physicians. The barber was on the first floor, and my violin teacher lived around the corner.

Going south along the streetcar line you ran into World Drug, Mr. Rothkovitch's pharmacy. His son became the famous artist, Mark Rothko. Next door was Goldstein's furniture and then came Mrs. Levine's fish market.

The Lair Hill Market at 2823 SW First Ave. is now a neighborhood restaurant. Leo Greenstein's aunt owned it and left it to her daughter and son-in-law, Esther and Slim Schulhaus. Slim was a Holocaust survivor and got his nickname from being slender.

Leo Greenstein: My great-uncle and Tanta Raizel owned the Lair Hill Market. It was an old-fashioned store where you told the grocer what you wanted, and he walked around and got it for you. They had a little room in back near the kitchen where we sat and talked.

Mike Scorcio: Sawmills operated up and down the Willamette River. Dad worked for the Clark-Wilson lumber company. Eventually, he got a job with the railroad that ran between Portland, Spokane and Seattle. He was in the section gang that repaired roadbeds. In the late afternoon, he came home carrying an eight-foot railroad tie on each shoulder. They weighed a ton! That was our winter heating supply.

Richard Falaschetti: My paternal grandfather worked in a sawmill down on Front Avenue and his wife, Modesta, did sewing and embroidery. In the '40s Grandpa had an Italian restaurant on Southeast Thirty Fourth Avenue and Powell Boulevard called Palm Gardens. He was the owner and the cook. I still use his chef's knife.

My maternal grandfather was from Horatio de Calabria where people were farmers and worked with stones. He started a cement contracting business in Portland. He and his men dug out basements before there were mechanized steam shovels. Sidewalks he built in Lair Hill still have his name engraved in them.

Jerry Stern: My father had foresight and established the third garage in Portland. It was on Fourth and Lincoln. In those days houses didn't have private garages so this was a safe place to leave your car at night. That garage stored 50 vehicles including the hearse for Shaarie Torah and popcorn wagons.

Frieda Cohen: She was a typical Jewish lady. That means she worked in the house, took care of her kids, did the washing, ironing, and shopping and went to shul on Yom Tov. That was it! There was no such thing as NOW, and they weren't looking for equality in the synagogue.

Their clothes were conservative, mid-calf. None of the women went bare in any way. I don't remember seeing Jewish women dressed unusually except for a few old ones who still wore a farchela on their head and floor-length dresses. One dear old lady like that was our neighbor. She ruled the roost. She was the boss.

Oscar Kirshner's business card. Courtesy Deborah Reinhardt Brandt.

Gussie Reinhardt: People today worry that women don't have enough say but believe me, the women of South Portland had everything to say. The wife got the husband's meager earnings and took care of budgeting. As a result, the women of South Portland ran the show.

Deborah Reinhardt Brandt: My grandfather took two horses and a buggy on his regular route. He picked up hides, pelts, tallow, and cascara bark and always brought back sugar cookies for Mom.

Gussie Reinhardt: Papa earned his living covering the countryside buying up hides and selling them to the Bissinger Hide and Fur Company in Portland. Sometimes he took my brother. He left on Monday morning, traveled to McMinnville, Aurora, Canby, and Salem, and started home on Thursday. He slept in haylofts or sometimes a farmer invited him to stay in his house. There were no hotels.

My mother kept my sister and me busy working because she helped my father a lot. Everything came in big flour sacks – feed for horses, potatoes, everything. They were expensive new but unusable if they were torn. Papa collected torn sacks and brought them to Mama who had golden hands. She sat outside in the sun and sewed those sacks so you couldn't even tell there was a patch.

Ernie Casciato: My grandmother was a tough cookie. She took in laundry and cleaned houses for people who lived in the Heights.

Richard Falaschetti: My maternal grandmother wore floral print dresses, aprons, shawls, woolen coats and little black pumps. Her hair was braided up on her head. The thing she enjoyed most was going shopping downtown once a week and visiting the Meier & Frank Department Store.

Joe Colasuonno: My father and grandfather had an employment agency where they recruited laborers for shipping and the railroad. In exchange the crews bought their groceries from our store. They all had their own cooks, and we boxed up food and shipped it to them.

Dad collected orders once a month by driving to extra houses and section gangs from here to Idaho. When I was six, I'd go with him sometimes. He'd let me sit on his lap and steer the car along the old Columbia Gorge highway. We stopped at parks and ate Italian tuna and loaves of fresh bread.

Fred Granata: My father was a stonemason, and jobs were hard to find. During the Depression he was out of work for an entire year. Then, in 1935 they started the WPA and in a short time he was one of two superintendents of stonework. My mother never worked outside the home. That was not the way they were brought up.

Italians dominated Portland's produce market, and Italian farmers leased what is now Ladd's Addition and eastward. In addition to the 10 or 15 acre farms, many people supplemented their income selling vegetables grown in their garden.

Farmers sold directly off their trucks at the Ranchers and Gardeners Association's early morning bazaar. Most customers owned stalls elsewhere in the city or were neighborhood peddlers.

Ernie Casciato: My father owned a restaurant on Produce Row called Tony and Don's. Today, it's the Produce Row Cafe [204 SE Oak Street]. It was a greasy spoon and mostly served breakfast since all those produce guys were down there by 4 A.M. Dad wound up running the Gresham dog track, and he was a [1]Columbus Record editor when I was little.

Fred Granata: The Lido and Monte Carlo [Southeast Eleventh Avenue and Belmont Street] were 24-hour-a-day Italian restaurants, and an early market was behind them. Farmers sold produce to brokers and peddlers.

That must have been a colorful scenario with the bargaining. It was also heartbreaking because the farmers woke at one in the morning, brought their produce to early market, and then worked in the farm until dinner time. A friend told me they slept between courses at meals.

The Yamhill Market extended along Southwest Yamhill Street between First and Fifth Avenue. Italians owned many of the open-air stalls.

Mike Scorcio: My mother did all her shopping downtown. She took the streetcar to stores or Yamhill Market stalls. I worked there as a boy. My dad ended up working for a farmer, and if he needed help in his stall, I was elected. Most truck farmers were Italian. They had small farms and would truck their produce to the market and rent a stall.

---

[1] The Columbus Record was a weekly Italian-American newspaper published in Portland 1930 to 1963.

During the Depression, wine making was common both for personal consumption and to sell. Several people interviewed remembered elaborate wine making facilities in their basement.

Richard Falaschetti: There was a movie theater on Grant and another on Lincoln but if you really wanted to enjoy yourself, you went to nightclubs. My dad told me that during Prohibition, there were places where they paid-off cops to let them know about upcoming raids.

People made home brew and wine, and some local police were paid off so there was an element of corruption but everyone was doing this. My grandfather made beer and sold it to city officials.

Carl Costanzo: My father bought 50 or 60 boxes of grapes when they came up from California every year. My job was to grind them. Our basement had a wine room carved into the rocks, and a natural spring kept the wine cool.

Joe Colasuonno: Every year a broker brought freight car loads of grapes from California. They parked on Southeast Third Avenue where the Sheridan Market is today. Word got out, and we went down there at night with lanterns. Each railroad car had a different type of grape, and we went from freight car to freight car tasting them. In 1926, Dad bought 200 20-pound boxes at $1 per box.

Of course, no law forbids selling grapes. The thing was not to let them know who you were and where you lived. Two blocks from home we switched off the headlights and coasted the rest of the way.

Next day we processed, and in the early 1920's that meant stomping grapes with rubber boots. We made over 500 gallons a year.

Leo Greenstein: Dad sold bottles to bootleggers during Prohibition. It was a good business.

Jack Rosen: A brothel operated on First and Hall. Girls tapped on the window to attract old Jews' attention as they left Shaarie Torah.

We heard that one old lady with a lot of rental property had made her money as a madam. One time a tenant screamed at her, "Mrs. so and so, don't get smart with me, I know you were a madam in the old days." She said, "You're damn right. Your father was my best customer."

Joe Colasuonno: The Chinese Consul was next to my grandfather's store. I'll never forget him. When he left, he gave me a footlocker full of fireworks.

A junk yard and prostitution home were across the street. The girls were nice. They bought groceries at our store.

When my dad opened his own store in 1936, another prostitution home operated across the street. A red light hung out front. These weren't streetwalkers. Looking at them, you would never know they were prostitutes.

Jerry Stern: My father-in-law told a story. When he was young, this guy offered to teach him to be a peddler. They drove to Medford where they bought leftover WWI scrap and then drove on to San Francisco where they sold it to a dealer. On the way back, they got as far as Sacramento and he said to my father-in-law, "Harry, this is hard work. My brother is a pimp in Portland and has an easy life. Here are the keys to the truck, it's yours -- just let me off. I'm going into a business like my brother's."

Organizations & Charities

Rose City Lodge meeting. Courtesy Nina Weinstein.

In 1910, Portland had three major Italian benevolent societies: Columbia Lodge, Bersaglieri-Columbia and Mazzini. Created to financially assist the Italian community, they doubled as social clubs.

By 1932, the city had 16 Italian organizations. Many met at the Italian Federation Hall on Southwest Fourth Avenue and Madison Street which had meeting rooms on first floor and a ballroom upstairs.

Today's Jewish Federation of Greater Portland began in 1919 when 13 organizations, many organized by South Portlanders, united to form the Federated Jewish Societies of Portland.

Joe Colasuonno: Dad was a founder of the Sons of Italy Portland Lodge. They started with over 400 charter members. A year later, women of the Sons of Italy organized and called themselves Ladies Rose City. They elected my mother president.

Fred Granata: In later years, the Tuscan Association and other organizations attracted 20 to 50 people. Today, Club Paesano is the most thriving Italian club. Most members once farmed in Ladd's Addition.

South Portland was a self-contained community, and people in the neighborhood formed organizations to help each other. In addition, German Jewish groups did much to assist the newcomers. For example, the National Council of Jewish Women started the Neighborhood House, and the First Hebrew Benevolent Society helped immigrants start businesses by providing loans and grants.

Gussie Reinhardt: When they came from Europe, they didn't rely on anyone else for help. They set up little organizations like the Ladies Free Loan Society. I went door-to-door collecting 25 cents a month from everyone in the area.

The Bikur Cholim Society was a quarter every month, too. That's Hebrew for taking care of the sick. They helped anyone who needed a doctor or had to go to the county hospital, which was right there in [what is now] Lair Hill Park.

Jack Rosen: My mother founded and was president of the local Ladies Free Loan Society. Nobody knew who borrowed money.

Frieda Cohen: My mother belonged to organizations like the Ladies Free Loan Society. They collected nickels and dimes at their silver tea and made funds available at no interest. It was anywhere from $50 to $100 -- $200 tops. They always got paid back. The wonderful thing was nobody knew who borrowed money. There was no blabbing.

Jewish Shelter Home, 1920. Photographer Brian McCabe, Courtesy SHPO.

In 1920, the Child Welfare Commission licensed the Jewish Shelter Home. Julius Meier, who became governor of Oregon, was the first president. Designed for the short-term residence of up to 12 children, many stayed for several years. Some children were orphans but most had at least one living parent who was too ill or poor to care for them. The Jewish community tried to integrate the children in school and community activities.

In 1935 or 1936, the shelter home moved to 1428 SW 12th Ave. Mrs. Evelyn Flanagan, a former Doernbecher hospital nurse, served as matron in both locations.

A parking lot replaced the new building but the beautiful original Jewish Shelter home on 4133 SW Corbett Ave. is a designated historic landmark.

Leo Greenstein: I knew some kids there. In 1935, I went to B'nai B'rith camp at Devil's Lake with kids from the orphanage. The Jewish community paid for them. The kids didn't say much about it but living in a home is not like having your own place.

Lair Hill Park was the site of the original Multnomah County Hospital. The hospital was originally a mansion owned by Charles E. Smith who donated the land and house to the city in 1909. When the hospital moved to Marquam Hill in 1923, the city demolished the mansion and the land became a public park.

Gussie Reinhardt: The county hospital was on [what is now] Lair Hill Park, and the nurses' residence was next door. When I was five or six my mother made up Shabbos baskets, and I brought them to neighbors who were in the hospital. The nurses wore little starched white aprons and caps. They opened the door, led me into the kitchen, and emptied the baskets.

In 1934, the Soviet government established a Jewish homeland in Siberia. Officially called the Jewish Autonomous Region (JAR), many referred to it by the area's capital city, Birobidzhan. About 18,000 Jews moved to the JAR from other parts of Russia and from Lithuania, Argentina, and the United States.

The Association for Jewish Colonization in the Soviet Union (ICOR) promoted awareness and raised funds for the project. One hundred ICOR chapters organized throughout the U.S. According to Oregonian newspaper accounts, the Portland chapter of ICOR met regularly during the mid-1930s at Congregation Linath Hazedek, the B'nai B'rith Building and the Neighborhood House.

Jerry Stern: One fellow believed in Birobidzhan, the Jewish homeland in Eastern Siberia. He founded the Portland chapter of ICOR. They held fund-raising dances or parties almost every other weekend.

The Workmen's Circle (Arbeiter Ring) started in New York City and became a national organization in 1900. Supporting the labor movement and closely tied to the Yiddish Press, they provided benefits such as sick care and burial service. They also established a Yiddish theater and Yiddish language schools.

Leo Greenstein: They went by the Yiddish name, Arbeiter Ring. It was a national organization and sort of left wing. My dad was the local branch secretary for 30 years. Gradually as conditions improved and the New Deal came in, the reason for their existence disappeared. They wanted sick benefits and worker education, things like that.

The sickening news about the Holocaust left immigrant families desperate to help those left behind in Europe.

Frieda Cohen: I started hearing about the Holocaust in 1938. Jewish leaders everywhere brought it to our attention. We were all outspoken, especially Rabbi Berkowitz of Temple Beth Israel. The community became tight, sticking together even more than before.

My mother and aunt saved money to buy clothes and sent them to their family in Poland. We never heard from them.

Eloise Durkheimer Spiegel: When my parents helped people escape Europe, we discovered wonderful relatives.

Founded in 1920, the Portland Chapter of Hadassah was the city's major Zionist organization. After the Holocaust, a Jewish homeland took on additional importance and meaning.

Gussie Reinhardt planting trees in Israel. Courtesy herself.

Gussie Reinhardt: I'll never forget it. It was 1947, and the United Nations was voting. Would they partition Palestine and create a Jewish state?

We stayed up all night listening to the radio. Once the UN voted YES!, the new country needed a name. Leaders like David Ben Gurian and Golda Meier chose Israel, which was perfect.

Houses of Worship

Congregation Shaarie Torah, Southwest First Avenue and Hall Street. Like everything in South Portland, the synagogue had a nickname, and it was better known as the First Street Shul. Courtesy Portland Development Commission.

It's hard to keep track of South Portland's synagogues as they moved and merged but names that come up include Ahavai Shalom, Ahavath Achim, Linath Hazedek, Shaarie Torah, Kesser Israel, Neveh Tzedek and Talmud Torah. The Reform congregation, Temple Beth Israel began above a downtown livery stable in 1858. By the early 1900s, they moved to their second synagogue at Southwest Twelfth Avenue and Main Street.

Italian South Portlanders worshipped at St. Lawrence Church at Southwest Third Avenue and Sheridan Street or St. Michael's, which still stands, at Southwest Fourth Avenue and Mill Street.

Harry Turtledove: My father and I went to South Portland on holidays. We'd sit with my maternal grandparents at Neveh Zedek and then walk to the First Street Shul to meet my great-grandfather. That was really Orthodox. The men sat with their shoes off, and I remember the sweaty feet.

Jerry Stern: Everyone and everything had a nickname even the synagogues. Linath Hazedek was the Kazatsker Shul, kazatsker being a Russian dance. Kesser Israel was the Meade Street Shul, Neveh Zedek the Sixth Street Shul and Ahavath Achim the Turkish Shul. Shaarie Torah was the First Street Shul, and they called the rabbi Royta Rov because he had red hair.

Daniel Labby: When my family moved to the east side they switched from Orthodox to Conservative. I was Bar Mitzvah'd in Conservative and confirmed in Reform at Congregation Beth Israel. That was the typical progression.

Frieda Cohen: We belonged to the First Street Shul. I didn't even know it had the name Shaarie Torah until I was an adult. Our basic religious training began at home which my mother kept strictly kosher. Although my father was not observant, he was knowledgeable, and everything in our home was religiously correct.

Kesser Israel Synagogue shorty before the congregation moved to their current location in Hillsdale. The building on Southwest Meade Street still stands and is now a church. Photo by author.

Gussie Reinhardt: My father belonged to the First Street Shul. When they took out their center bimah and became a little more liberal, he and several other men pulled out. They bought the Immanuel Baptist Church and formed Kesser Israel.

My father became president of the synagogue in 1924 and remained so for 40 years. He sat on the bimah in a big chair facing east [toward Jerusalem] and my mother sat in the balcony where he could see her.

During urban renewal people asked why he hung onto Kesser Israel. He said, "There must be one place in Oregon where an Orthodox Jew can pray."

Richard Falaschetti: My grandmother's family were fisherman from Bari in Southern Italy. She and my grandfather had an arranged marriage, I imagine at St. Michael's Church. St. Michael's was the focal point of the Italian community. Everything happened there.

Italian immigrants built the Church of St. Michael the Archangel, photo by author.

Ernie Casciato: When my grandmother had cataracts in the '30s and '40s, she prayed to Saint Lucy of the Eye for a successful operation. Afterward, my mother and aunt started the Santa Lucia Guild at St. Michael's with the goal of raising money for the church.

Fred Granata: My parents dressed up when they went downtown. My father wore a suit and tie, and my mother wore a hat and white gloves. *Bella figura*, the importance of always looking good, was a common trait among Italians. I think that's why St. Michael's is such an attractive church. In those days, Portland Catholics mostly built small wooden churches which were not *bella figura*.

I was baptized and married in St. Michael's along with all my relatives. Technically we're parishioners even if we don't attend because it's a Vatican designated Italian National Church.

Ernie Casciato: At the end of her life my mother was sick. When I asked if she were afraid to die, she said, no, she was ready but worried how she'd look to my father. He was only 65 when he died and here she was 89.

Urban Renewal

Unidentified woman outside Korsun's Delicatessen during urban renewal. Courtesy Portland Development Commission.

In 1958, Portland voted to create the South Auditorium Urban Renewal District and bulldozers demolished 54 blocks of the immigrant community north of Southwest Arthur Street.

Frieda Cohen: I was always sorry to see the old neighborhood go. As people worked and gained in monetary stature, they moved. The east side migration went on for 20 years and suddenly my generation turned back to the west side.

Harry Turtledove: South Portland served its purpose in terms of a residence. It was an older neighborhood with small houses, and there was a steady decline in population. People moved to Laurelhurst and Irvington. They moved up.

Gussie Reinhardt chaired the committee that prevented the demolition of the area south of Southwest Arthur Street. Known as Lair Hill, it is the one section of Old South Portland that escaped urban renewal.

Gussie Reinhardt: Five or six synagogues were in South Portland when HUD and the freeways came. Urban renewal got busy burning down, tearing up and buying the little homes where people had lived for 50 years. They paid them 95 cents a foot. The high rises went up, and land values skyrocketed. They promised to help those displaced people find replacement homes. They never did. So many I knew struggled. They were not young.

The darling little houses in Lair Hill could have also been lost. Urban renewal and the Portland Development Commission wanted to tear down the triangle from Arthur to Curry Street and Barbur Boulevard. The community chose a board, and we worked every Wednesday night for four years. Finally, the administration changed, and HUD went away

Map of South Portland

This map was created using Sanborn Maps, Portland City Directories and census data.

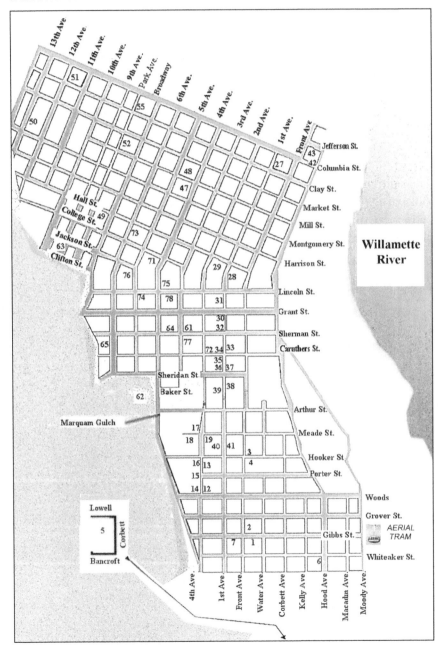

TABLE 1: Key to map on page 64

1.	Gevurtz Hall
2.	Wintler's Drugs
3.	Manley Center *
4.	Failing School after 1913 *
5.	Shelter Home before 1935 *
6.	Mike Scorcio's home *
7.	Leo Greenstein's home
12.	Neighborhood House*
13.	Daniel Labby's grandfather's home *
14.	Nurse's Residence *
15.	Lair Hill Park
16.	South Portland Library *
17.	Ada Layton's home *
18.	Gussie Reinhardt's home
19.	Kesser Israel Synagogue *

27.	Garibaldi Grocery
28.	Shaarie Torah Synagogue
29.	Jack Rosen's home
30.	1st Ave. (Grant St.) Theater
31.	Portland Kosher Meat Market
32.	Cottell's Drugstore & Dr. Labby's home
33.	Linath Hazedek Synagogue
34.	Mrs. Levine's Fish Market
35	Korsun's Deli
36	Calistro & Halperin's Deli
37	Mosler's Bakery
38	Portland Kosher Market
39	Southern Hotel
40	Lair Hill Market*
41	Jermolowske home *
42	Acme Junk
43	Pacific Bottle

47.	St. Michael's Church and Academy*
48.	St. Mary's Academy
49.	Shattuck School *
50	B'nai B'rith Building
51	Jewish Shelter home after 1935
52	Lincoln High
55	Temple Ahavai Shalom
61	St. Lawrence Church
62	Duniway Park *
63	Frieda Cohen's home
64	Richard Falaschetti's father's home
65	Fred Granata's aunt's home *
71	Mrs. Neusihan's Pickles
72	Martell's Grocery

73	Neveh Tsevak Talmud Torah
74	Jerry Stern's home
75	Fourth Street Garage
76	Richard Matza's home
77	Congregation Ahavath Achim
78	Lincoln Theater

*The original structure is still standing. See Table 2 for the address.

	Table 2	Addresses of structures that remain.
3	Manly Center	2828 SW Front Ave. at the corner of Front Ave. and Hooker Street.
4	Failing School after 1913	049 SW Porter St. at the corner of Naito Parkway and Porter St.
5	Jewish Shelter Home before 1935	4133 SW Corbett Ave. between Lowell and Bancroft St.
6	Mike Scorcio's home	3405 SW Hood Ave at the corner of Hood Ave. and Whiteaker St.
12	Neighborhood House	3030 SW 2nd Ave. on the corner of Second Ave. and Woods St.
13	Daniel Labby's first home	2922 SW 2nd Ave. between Hooker and Porter St.
14	Nurse's Residence	The corner of SW Second Avenue and Woods St.
15	Lair Hill Park	SW 2nd Ave. between Hooker and Woods St.
16	South Portland Library	2909 SW 2nd Ave. at the corner of Second Ave. and Hooker St.
17	Ada Calof Layton's home	2737 SW 2nd Ave. at the NW corner of SW Second Ave. and Meade St.

19	Kesser Israel Synagogue	136 SW Meade St. at the SE corner of Second Ave. and Meade St.
40	Lair Hill Market	2823 SW 1st Ave. between Meade and Hooker St.
41	Jermolowske home	2818 SW 1st Ave. between Meade and Hooker St.
47	St. Michael's Church	424 SW Mill St. at the corner of Fourth Ave. and Mill St.
49	Shattuck School	1914 SW Park Ave. between Hall and College St.
62	Duniway Park	3050 SW Terwilliger Blvd at the corner of 4th Ave and Sheridan St.
65	Fred Granata's Aunt's home.	2323 SW 6th Ave. and Caruthers St.

Glossary

baccala: salt cod sold by the slab.

bimah: elevated area in a Jewish synagogue where the person reading the Torah aloud stands.

bella figura: literally, a beautiful figure; loosely translated, the importance of always looking good.

Beth Midrash: school for advanced Torah study.

Bintel Brief: advice column in the Jewish Daily Forward newspaper.

bocce bal: lawn bowling.

cheder: Jewish religious school for elementary school students.

farchela: kerchief

fatsheyle: Yiddish for shawl or kerchief.

goyim: non-Jew.

knaidlach: dumplings made of matzoh meal.

knishes: dough stuffed with potato, meat, cheese, or kasha and fried.

Ladino: a language derived mainly from Spanish and Hebrew and spoken by Sephardic Jews.

matzoh: unleavened bread.

Midrash: commentaries on the Hebrew Scriptures compiled between 400 and 1200 A.D.

mikvah: ritual bath.

minyan: quorum of 10 Jewish adults (traditionally males) required for religious service.

Rosh Hashanah: Jewish New Year.

Shavous: holiday that commemorates Moses accepting the Torah on Mt. Sinai.

shochet: authorized kosher butcher.

semichka: sunflower seeds.

Shabbos: the Sabbath.

shammes: synagogue caretaker.

Shavous: holiday that commemorates Moses receiving the Torah at Mount Sinai.

shtetl: small village in Eastern Europe.

tanta: Yiddish for aunt.

tefillin: leather boxes containing biblical verses worn on the arm and head during morning prayer.

Tisha B'Av: Jewish fast day commemorating the destruction of the temples in Jerusalem.

traif: non-kosher food.

Yiddish: a language derived mainly from German and Hebrew and spoken by Ashkenazic Jews.

Yom Tov: holidays.

zaydeh: Yiddish for grandfather.

Chapter Notes

Front cover photo Anna and Oscar Kirshner with their two eldest children Ora and Hyman. Both children were born in Russia. Their other two children Gussie and Isadore were born in Oregon. Courtesy of their granddaughter Deborah Reinhardt Brandt.

Introduction

- Population statistics are from Lowenstein, Steven; The Jews of Oregon: 1850-1950; pg. 92 and Gould, Charles F; Portland Italians, 1880-1920; Oregon Historical Quarterly; Sept. 1976; Volume LXXVII; pg. 246.

Coming to Portland

- Glazier, Jack; Dispersing the Ghetto, The Relocation of Jewish Immigrants Across America; Cornell University Press; 1998; ISBN: 0-8014-3522-6.

- Center for Jewish History, Industrial Removal Records; www.cjh.org.

- Rockaway, Robert A.; Words of the Uprooted; Cornell University Press; 1198; ISBN: 0-8014-8550-9.

- Relieving Congestion in the Russian Jewish Quarter; New York Times; Jan. 20. 1907; pg. SM3.

- Calof, Rachel; Rachel Calof's Story: Jewish Homesteader on the Northern Plains; Indiana University Press; September 22, 1995; ISBN-13 978-0253209863.

- American Jewish Historical Archives Manuscript Catalog; Woodbine Agricultural School (1893-1927); Baron de Hirsch Fund (1870-1935); Baron de Hirsch Trade School (1890-1935); Industrial Removal Office (1899-1922); www.jewishgen.org (search: AJHS Manuscript Catalog).

- Lee, Samuel J.; Moses of the New World, The Work of Baron de Hirsch; A.S. Barnes & Co; 1970; ISBN: 0498073785; pg. 273 - 282.

The Established German Jews

- An Appeal in Aid of the Sufferers from the Kishineff Outrage; Jewish Tribune; May 15, 1903; #13.

- Jews in Romania and Poland Alarmed; New York Times; May 21, 1903.

- Judge, Edward H.; Easter in Kishinev: Anatomy of a Pogrom; New York University Press; New York; 1992.

Growing Up

- Where Ghosts Dwelt; The Oregon Journal; Jan. 1, 1952; Section 3, pg. 6.

- New Settlement Opens; The Oregonian; April 1, 1929; Section H2.

- An Appeal for Apostates; The Neighborhood; A monthly publication of the Neighborhood House; April, 1920; Volume 1, #11; pg. 1.

- Lowenstein, Steven; The Jews of Oregon 1859 - 1950; Jewish Historical Society of Oregon; Portland; 1987; pg. 108,172.

- Marquam Gulch to be used as Dumping Place for Garbage; The Oregonian; May 30, 1914; pg. 12.

- Marquam's Gulch Garbage Plans Are Now Discontinued; The Oregonian; Oct. 24, 1914; pg. 18.

- Park Plan Favored, Citizens in Other Parts Give Way to South Portland; The Oregonian; Sept. 24, 1916; Section1, pg. 20.

- Work is Promised on Duniway Park, City Council Gives Pledge Fill Will Be Rushed; The Oregonian; April 14, 1923, pg. 22.

- The Children's Park; The Oregon Journal; April 16, 1923; pg. 8.

- Jimmy Berg oral history; Oregon Jewish Museum.

At Work

- Gould, Charles F; Portland Italians, 1880-1920; Oregon Historical Quarterly; Sept. 1976; Volume LXXVII.

- Colasuonno, Joe; Club Paesano, 40 Years; privately published.

- Portland Italians: The Early Settlers; The Oregonian; Jul. 9, 1972, pg. 6.

Organizations & Charities

- Gould, Charles F; Portland Italians, 1880-1920; Oregon Historical

- Quarterly; Sept. 1976; Volume LXXVII; pg. 257.

- Colasuonno, Joe; Club Paesano 40 Years; privately published.

- Orphan Home Fund $5000, Jews to Erect Structure on Corbett Street; The Oregonian; Jan. 4, 1920; pg. 2.

- Jewish Shelter Home Minutes; Oregon Jewish Museum.

- Polk's Portland City Directory, 1933 - 1938.

- Stalin's Forgotten Zion, An Illustrated History;
  Swarthmore College; University of California Press;
  www.swarthmore.edu/Home/News/biro/

- Polk's Portland City Directory, Classified Business
  Section; Societies,1938-40.

Sources

Oregon Jewish Museum

- *An Appeal for Apostates*; The Neighborhood; A monthly publication of the Neighborhood House; April, 1920; Volume 1, #11.

- Jewish Shelter Home minutes.

- oral history collection.

- photo collection.

Oregon Historical Society

- Gould, Charles F; *Portland Italians*, 1880-1920; Oregon Historical Quarterly; Sept. 1976; Volume LXXVII.

- *An Appeal in Aid of the Sufferers from the Kishineff Outrage*; Jewish Tribune; May 15, 1903.

- Portland City Archives photo collection.

- Portland Development Commission photo collection.

- Polk's Portland City Directory.

- U.S. Census, 1910, 1920, 1930.

- Portland Public School Archives.

The Oregonian

- *County Hospital Model Institution*; March 22, 1912, pg. 15.

- *Marquam Gulch to be used as Dumping Place for Garbage*; The Oregonian; May 30, 1914; pg. 12.

- *Marquam's Gulch Garbage Plans Are Now Discontinued;* The Oregonian; Oct. 24, 1914; pg. 18.

- *Park Plan Favored, Citizens in Other Parts Give Way to South Portland*; Oregonian; Sept. 24, 1916; Section 1, pg. 20.

- *All Junk to be Stamped*; Jan. 11, 1918; pg. 4.

- *Orphan Home Fund $5000, Jews to Erect Structure on Corbett Stree*t; Jan. 4, 1920

- *Work is Promised on Duniway Park, City Council Gives Pledge Fill Will Be Rushed*; April 14, 1923, pg. 22.

- *City Ordinance Upheld, Regulation Covering Peddlers and Solicitors Probably Will Be Taken to the Supreme Court*; April 22, 1924, pg. 6

- *New Settlement Opens*; April 1, 1929

- *Know Your City, Italian Stock in Portland Growing*; April 20, 1930.

- *New Officers Seated by Junk Peddlers*; Dec. 21, 1934; pg. 2.

- *Portland Italians: The Early Settlers*; Jul. 9, 1972, pg. 6.

- *Portland's Italian Heritage Celebrated*; August 23, 1993.

- Stern, Harry; *Limits Opportunities for Young Men and Women;* Sept. 1, 2000.

Oregon Journal

- *Closing of County Hospital is Urged* by Rufus Holman; Nov. 29, 1915; pg. 2.

- *Site of the Old Country Hospital is to be Turned* into Park; Jan. 2, 1919; pg. 8.

- *The Children's Park*; April 16, 1923; pg. 8.

- *Open House is Held by Junk Dealers Here*; Oct. 11, 1928.

- *Where Ghosts Dwelt;* Jan. 1, 1952; S3, p6.

- *Portland's Gypsy Problem*; Dec. 25, 1956.

- Crick, Rolla; *Will Our Gypsies Conform*; Dec. 26, 1956.

- Moyles, Mike; B. Mike's Lowdown: *Portland Gypsy Quarter Could Out-Fame SF Chinatown, LA Alvera St.*; Jan. 6, 1957.

Pacific Historical Review

- Toll, William; *Ethnicity and Stability: The Italians and Jews of South Portland, 1900-1940*; Pacific Historical Review; Vol. 54; May 1985.

New York Times Historical Archives

- *Jews in Romania and Poland Alarmed;* May 21, 1903.

- *Relieving Congestion in the Russian Jewish Quarter*; Jan. 20. 1907.

Websites

- Center for Jewish History; research, selected finding aids; Industrial Removal Office records; Baron de Hirsch Fund Records; www.cjh.org.

- Ellis Island Database, Stephen Morse one-step tools; www.jewishgen.org.

- Stalin's Forgotten Zion, An Illustrated History; Swarthmore College; University of California Press; www.swarthmore.edu/Home/News/biro/

- The Sam Aseez Museum of Woodbine Heritage; www.thesam.org/

Books

- Colasuonno, Joe; *Club Paesano 40 Years*, 1955 - 1995; privately published.

- David, Jay; *Growing Up Jewish in America, An Anthology*; William Morrow and Company; New York; ISBN: 0688128246.

- Fenyvesi, Charles; *When the World Was Whole, Three Centuries of Memories*; Viking; New York; 1990; ISBN: 0670831808.

- Glazier, Jack; *Dispersing the Ghetto, The Relocation of Jewish Immigrants Across America*; Cornell University Press; 1998; ISBN: 0-8014-3522-6.

- Golden, Harry; *A Bintel Brief, Sixty Years of Letters from the Lower East Side to the Jewish Daily Forward*; Doubleday; New York; 1971; LCC 71-139047.

- Granata, Fred A.; *The 100 Year Celebration of the Church of Saint Michael the Archangel*, 1894-1994; 1994; privately published.

- Hoffman, Eva; *Shtetl, The Life and Death of a Small Town and the World of Polish Jews*; Houghton Mifflin Company; Boston; 1997; ISBN: 0395822955.

- Howe, Irving; *World of Our Fathers;* Schocken; New York; 1989; ISBN: 080520928.

- Judge, Edward H.; *Easter in Kishinev: Anatomy of a Pogrom*; New York University Press; New York; 1992.

- Lee, Samuel J.; *Moses of the New World, The Work of Baron de Hirsch*; A.S. Barnes & Co; 1970; ISBN: 0498073785.

- Lowenstein, Steven; *The Jews of Oregon 1859 - 1950*; Jewish Historical Society of Oregon; Portland; 1987; ISBN: 0961978619.

- Calof, Rachel; *Rachel Calof's Story: Jewish Homesteader on the Northern Plains*; Indiana University Press; September 22, 1995; ISBN-13 978-0253209863

- Rockaway, Robert A.; *Words of the Uprooted*; Cornell University Press; 1198; ISBN: 0-8014-8550-9.

- Sydney; Stahl; Weinberg; *The World of Our Mothers*; University of North Carolina Press; Chapel Hill; 1988; ISBN: 0807817627.

- Toll, William; *The Making of an Ethnic Middle Class*; State University of N.Y. Press; 1982; ISBN 0873956095

About the Author

All four of Polina Olsen's grandparents immigrated to America from Eastern Europe. When she learned that a neighborhood near her was once an immigrant community, she took photos of it and asked a 96-year-old woman who grew up there to identify the buildings. From there she interviewed many others with roots in South Portland and pieced together stories about life before the 1960's urban renewal project destroyed the neighborhood.

Polina gave tours of South Portland for more than a decade and wrote a "Looking Back" column for Oregon's Jewish newspaper, The Jewish Review. She lives in Portland with her husband and two cats.

Other books by Polina Olsen:

- A Walking Tour of Historic Jewish Portland.

- The Downtown Jews: A Walking Tour Through Portland's Early Business District.

- Stories from Jewish Portland.

- Portland in the 1960s: Stories from the Counterculture.

Index

Monte Carlo, 50
Mosler's Bakery, 26, 46, 66
Mrs. Levine's fish market, 47
Mrs. Neusihan's pickles, 46
Multnomah County Hospital, 35, 55

National Council of Jewish Women, 28, 54
Neighborhood House, 26, 28, 30, 65
Neveh Zedek Talmud Torah, 23
newspapers, selling, 26
North Dakota, 16
Nurse's Residence, 65

Octagonal Club, 40

Palm Gardens, 47
Passover, 40
population, 1
Porter, Fannie, 33
Portland Development Commission, 63
Produce Row, 50
Prohibition, 51
prostitution, 52

Queen Esther's Daughters, 32

Rachel Calof's Story, 16
railroad, 17, 47

Ranchers and Gardeners Association, 50
Reinhardt, Gussie, 8, 27, 29, 30, 36, 37, 40, 44, 46, 48, 54, 55, 57, 60, 63
Rockaway, 38
Roma, 21
Romaniote Jews, 7
Rosen, Jack, 9, 39, 52, 54
Rothko, Mark, 47

sanitary fill method, 35
sawmills, 47
Schneiderman's, 9
Scorcio, Mike, 9, 15, 20, 27, 31, 34, 36, 41, 47, 50
Seaside, 38
Selling, Ben, 13, 14
Shattuck School, 33
shochet, 9, 11
silent movies, 39
smokers, 21
Sons of Italy, 54
South Parkway Lodge, 30
Spiegel, Eloise Durkheimer, 10, 23, 29, 38, 57
St. Ignatius Church, 5
St. Lawrence Church, 58
St. Lawrence School, 34
St. Mary's Academy, 34
St. Michael's Church, 58, 61, 67
St. Michael's School, 34

Made in the USA
Coppell, TX
04 May 2022